DEFEND **AND** PROTECT

POLICE FORCE

Geoff Barker

Gareth Stevens
PUBLISHING

Please visit our website, **www.garethstevens.com**.
For a free color catalog of all our high-quality books,
call toll free 1-800-542-2595 or fax 1-877-542-2596.

Cataloging-in-Publication Data

Barker, Geoff.
Police force / by Geoff Barker.
p. cm. — (Defend and protect)
Includes index.
ISBN 978-1-4824-4110-9 (pbk.)
ISBN 978-1-4824-4111-6 (6-pack)
ISBN 978-1-4824-4114-7 (library binding)
1. Police — Juvenile literature. I. Barker, Geoff, 1963-. II. Title.
HV7922.B37 2016
363.2—d23

First Edition

Published in 2016 by
Gareth Stevens Publishing
111 East 14th Street, Suite 349
New York, NY 10003

© 2016 Gareth Stevens Publishing

Produced by Calcium
Editors: Sarah Eason and Jennifer Sanderson
Designers: Paul Myerscough and Simon Borrough
Picture research: Jennifer Sanderson

Picture credits: Department of Defense (DoD): Spc. Jillian Munyon 39; Dreamstime: 1000words 38,
Guruxox 30, Kbiros 17, Mediaonela 23, Photographerlondon 3, 20, 33, Stefano Inti 43, Victor Moussa
35; Shutterstock: A Katz 16, Africa Studio 8, Arindambanerjee 4, Bikeriderlondon 15, 32, P Cruciatti 12,
Rachel Donahue 5, Derek Hatfield 14, Fresnel 5b, 9b, 11b, 15b, 17b, 18b, 21b, 23b, 27b, 29b, 33b,
35b, 41b, Henrik Lehnerer 6, Jiri Hera 21, John Roman Images 10, 19, 24, 36–37, Larry St. Pierre 28,
Frederic Legrand / COMEO 34, LukaTDB 9, Maria Bell 7b, 13b, 21b, 31b, 36b, 43b, Monkey Business
Images 27, NSC Photography 13; US Army: Spc Steven K. Young 26; US Navy: Mass Communication
Specialist 3rd Class Kristopher Kirsop 41, 45; Wikimedia Commons: Dynamicentry 102 7, Fiatswat800
40, Lance Cpl. Cory D. Polom 22, Master Sgt. Donald Sparks 1, 42.

Printed in the United States of America

CPSIA compliance information: Batch #CW16GS: For further information contact
Gareth Stevens, New York, New York at 1-800-542-2595.

Contents

CHAPTER 1:
Law and Order

Police officers form a wall with their riot shields at a public protest in Toronto, Canada. They are also armed.

Who is brave enough to stand up against criminals who break the law? Imagine facing an armed robber alone and without backup. Police officers find themselves in these kinds of situations all the time. It is their job to maintain law and order on the streets and keep the peace in communities.

Police officers have three main functions that help define their work. First, they seek to maintain order: making sure people can carry on with their lives normally. Second, they are law enforcement officers, ensuring that no laws are being broken. Third, the police serve the general public. These important functions are connected to one another and all are equally important to every member of the police force, from a patrol officer to the sheriff.

Keeping the Peace

Members of the police force work together in teams to help keep the peace in our communities. When a crime is committed, police officers take statements from witnesses to investigate what has happened. They may also inform the public about issues and concerns, such as visiting a school to talk about the dangers of drug use. This book will explain the different aspects and roles of the police.

Under arrest

THINK LIKE A LAW ENFORCEMENT OFFICER

Modern law enforcement officers have a difficult job. They have to work different shifts, day or night. Officers need to balance all kinds of duties. One day they might be visiting a school, the next they may be acting as counselors, called in to deal with a dangerous argument in a home. Officers need to be skilled in dealing with many different people.

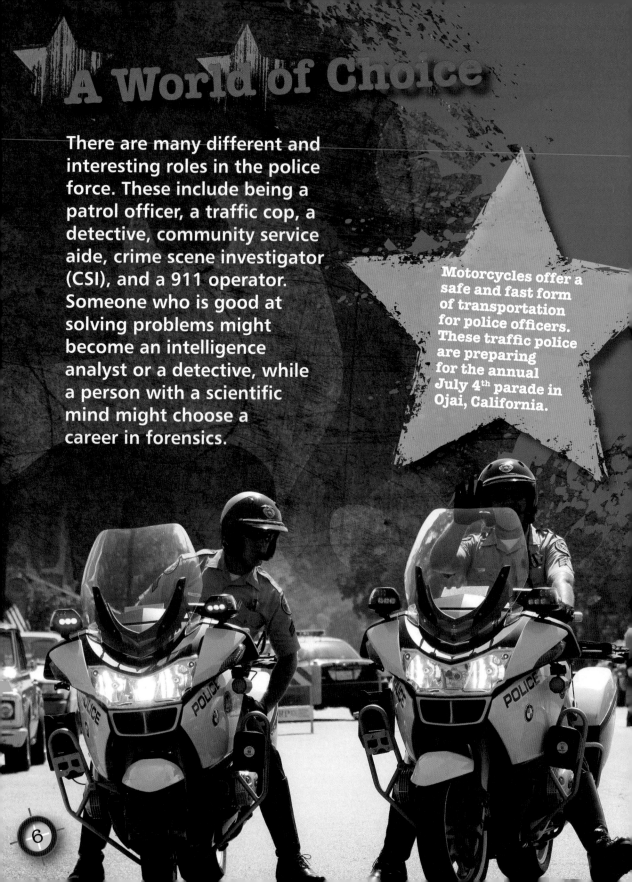

A World of Choice

There are many different and interesting roles in the police force. These include being a patrol officer, a traffic cop, a detective, community service aide, crime scene investigator (CSI), and a 911 operator. Someone who is good at solving problems might become an intelligence analyst or a detective, while a person with a scientific mind might choose a career in forensics.

Motorcycles offer a safe and fast form of transportation for police officers. These traffic police are preparing for the annual July 4th parade in Ojai, California.

Solving Cases

Detectives are important police investigators. Their role is to find out information about crimes and to use these facts to figure out who committed the crimes. Some detectives oversee teams of police officers who help them solve particular cases. Homicide detectives specialize in piecing together intelligence from murders.

Intelligence analysts search for information, perhaps using computer records, to help study particular crimes. They might look for links between different cases. They can then recommend ways to stop additional problems happening in the same neighborhood.

Detective's shield

THINK LIKE A 911 OPERATOR

A 911 operator is a frontline specialist. This highly trained operator takes calls from the general public and has to keep calm throughout, especially when dealing with an emergency. The operator must think and act quickly. They follow a script, which includes questions such as: What is your emergency? Where are you? What is your name? Using the answers to these questions, the operator then figures out what emergency service is required. Depending on the type of emergency the operator is dealing with, they may also ask: Are you hurt? If talking to a child, the operator needs to find out the child's age to help figure out what the child should do next.

Crime Scene Investigations

A CSI may be called out to the place where an incident has occurred, at any time of the day or night. This is how many police investigations start. The CSI goes quickly to the scene of the crime. Their first job will be to protect any evidence. The CSI will do an initial walk-through at the crime scene, taking care not to disturb any vital evidence.

Finding Evidence

CSIs need to be organized and methodical individuals who work well as part of a team. CSIs, as the forensic experts present at the scene of a crime, must make sure the team does not overlook any evidence, and that whatever is found is not damaged or destroyed. Evidence can include fingerprints, footprints, tire imprints, fibers, materials, hair, and any other biological evidence, such as blood or saliva.

Whether they have an arch, a whorl, a simple loop, or a double loop, fingerprints are unique. This is why CSIs check the crime scene for prints.

Physical evidence might be found at the scene of a crime or on a victim's body. The entire investigation depends on what a CSI finds, so it is vital that this evidence is protected. The CSI writes a detailed report about the collection of evidence. Anything found at the crime scene is then taken to the forensic laboratory where it is analyzed by technicians such as forensic chemists.

Protecting evidence

THINK LIKE A CSI

There are three stages of CSI work: identifying the scene, documenting the scene, and collecting any evidence. To do their job, CSIs often examine unpleasant incidents. They need to prepare themselves to deal with all sorts of difficult sights, including dead bodies at crime scenes. CSIs must remain calm and professional, making sure they document the scene with care. They will take photographs, sketch the scene, take measurements, and document any evidence that is removed from the scene—taking notes about what the item is and its precise location.

TAKE THE TEST!

Could you be a law enforcement officer?

Find out if you have what it takes to be a law enforcement officer. Use the information you have read so far to answer the following questions:

Q1. Name two out of the three main functions of police officers.

Q2. What do homicide detectives specialize in?

Q3. In the United States, who takes emergency calls from the general public?

Q4. What does CSI stand for?

Q5. What is the first thing a CSI must do with evidence at a crime scene?

Q6. Name two ways of documenting a crime scene.

Q7. Name two types of evidence that can be found at a crime scene.

ANSWERS

Q1. Any two of the following: maintaining order, enforcing law, serving the general public

Q2. Solving murders

Q3. 911 operators

Q4. Crime scene investigator

Q5. Make sure it is protected

Q6. Any two of the following: taking photographs, sketching the scene, taking detailed measurements, and taking notes

Q7. There are all sorts of evidence, including fingerprints, footprints, tire imprints, fibers, materials, hair, and other biological evidence such as blood and saliva

CHAPTER 2:
On Patrol

Uniformed police officers have to be alert at all times. They need to be prepared to think and act quickly in an emergency. In this job, events can take place very quickly and the officer must be ready to respond.

A police officer guards a public building during a royal visit in London, England.

Emergency Call!

Patrol officers usually work in pairs to ensure each other's safety and the safety of the community. These trained officers need to answer all emergency calls from their radio. Every day can provide any number of different situations to deal with, such as traffic violations, fights, thefts, and even shootings.

The officers called to a crime scene are usually those who are nearest to the incident. At the crime scene, they talk to anyone directly involved, and they also interview any witnesses. Police officers must listen, take notes, and make sure that the neighborhood is calm once more before they leave to return to the police station. At the station, they fill in paperwork relating to the incident. When that is completed, and if there are no emergencies to respond to, the officers will head back out on patrol.

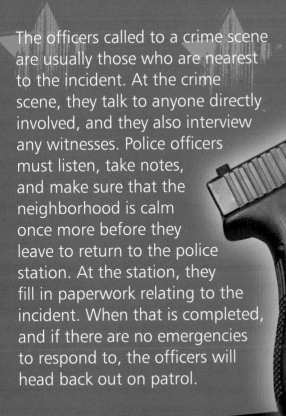

Gun and bullet cartridge

THINK LIKE AN ARMED PATROL OFFICER

In some countries, such as United Kingdom, Ireland, Iceland, Norway, and New Zealand, police officers are typically unarmed when they are on patrol. In the United States, however, patrol officers carry firearms. In 2013, the entire Los Angeles Police Department (LAPD) started to use the Smith & Wesson Military & Police (M&P) 9 handgun. The Remington 870 is a favored shotgun, manufactured by the United States' oldest and largest producer of rifles and shotguns. Carrying, and being prepared to use firearms in certain situations, is one of the responsibilities of being an armed patrol officer.

Fighting Crime

Over the last 15 years in the United States, figures for breaking and entering have stayed quite constant, at around 2 million per year. In 2013, more than 1,928,000 incidents of breaking and entering were committed. There were also more than 345,000 robberies (taking the property of another person). Patrol officers have to deal with many armed robbery incidents. Sometimes, by simply being on patrol on the streets, officers can help cut down on the number of incidents in their community.

Breaking and entering

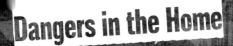

Dangers in the Home

If a dispute in a home occurs, officers will often attend the scene in pairs to support each other and deal with the people involved in the dispute. When they arrive at the scene, they will attempt to calm the situation. They will try to keep people away from the kitchen, where there may be knives, and the bedroom, where people often keep their firearms. While they deal with the situation, police officers must think of their own safety, as well as that of the people involved.

Domestic disputes require careful handling. Police officers, often working together in pairs, will need to deal with emotional people.

THINK LIKE A PATROL OFFICER

Whether dealing with a domestic dispute or a property crime, the patrol officer must think quickly. If dealing with a robbery, patrol officers will question the owners of the stolen goods, as well as people in the neighborhood. They will ask questions such as: What was taken? Did the owners and witnesses notice anyone unusual at that time of day? Are there any known thieves in the area? Do the owners suspect anyone? The police officers will then piece together all the information to figure out what happened.

Under Threat

Patrol officers sometimes deal with violent crimes, including homicide, robbery, and aggravated assault (usually with a deadly weapon). However, violent crimes have been steadily dropping in the United States over the past 20 years, since peaking at more than 1,930,000 separate incidents in 1992. In 2013, just more than 1,160,000 violent crimes were committed. Homicide figures have also fallen—from 23,760 in 1992 to 14,196 in 2013.

Lethal Force

According to statistics from the Federal Bureau of Investigation (FBI), guns are the preferred murder weapon: they are used in up to three-quarters of all homicides. In the face of extreme violence, or even the threat of violence, patrol officers have extensive training to ensure they respond correctly. They are taught how to speak calmly to an attacker. If this approach fails, officers may have to use force, so they learn self-defense techniques. Police officers learn how to disarm an attacker and make weapons safe quickly. They also weigh up whether to use lethal force: if they have to shoot to kill

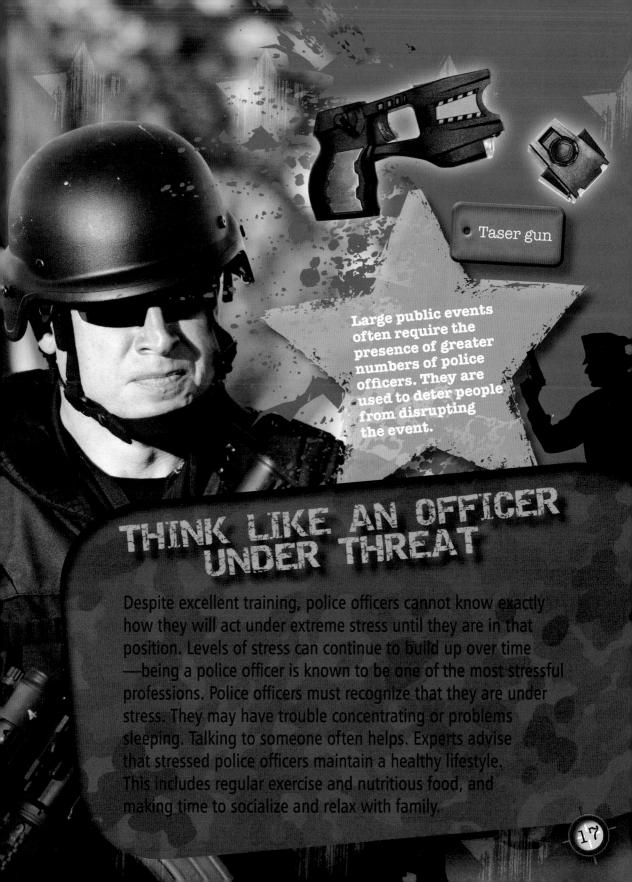

Taser gun

Large public events often require the presence of greater numbers of police officers. They are used to deter people from disrupting the event.

THINK LIKE AN OFFICER UNDER THREAT

Despite excellent training, police officers cannot know exactly how they will act under extreme stress until they are in that position. Levels of stress can continue to build up over time —being a police officer is known to be one of the most stressful professions. Police officers must recognize that they are under stress. They may have trouble concentrating or problems sleeping. Talking to someone often helps. Experts advise that stressed police officers maintain a healthy lifestyle. This includes regular exercise and nutritious food, and making time to socialize and relax with family.

TAKE THE TEST!

Could you be a patrol officer?

Are you observant enough to be a patrol officer? Check if you have been paying attention by answering these questions:

Q1. After an incident, which patrol officer is usually called first?

Q2. After an incident, who does a patrol officer interview?

Q3. Name three countries where police officers are unarmed.

Q4. Which handgun do officers in the LAPD use?

Q5. Around how many million incidents of breaking and entering are committed in the United States every year?

Q6. At a domestic dispute, why does the patrol officer try to avoid the kitchen?

Q7. What term is used for the act of shooting to kill?

ANSWERS

Q1. The patrol officer nearest to the incident
Q2. Anyone directly involved, as well as any witnesses
Q3. Any three of the following: Ireland, Iceland, Norway, New Zealand, and United Kingdom
Q4. Smith & Wesson Military & Police (M&P)
Q5. Around 2 million
Q6. Because knives are found there
Q7. Lethal force

CHAPTER 3:
Training

Young recruits train at their local police academy. The training usually lasts only 18 weeks, but it is very intense, both physically and mentally. Recruits spend time in the classroom and in the gym. They learn that police officers need to stay neutral and calm in difficult and dangerous situations.

Weapons training is a vital part of police training. At the firing range, an experienced instructor gives officers advice on improving their aim.

Handling Weapons

Gym work includes learning vital self-defense skills. Recruits also learn how and when it is appropriate to use force. The trainees find out how to subdue a suspect quickly, as well as helping the injured and performing first aid. It may seem exciting for a recruit to learn how to handle many different firearms for the first time, but as part of their training, young trainees discover first and foremost how to be safe around weapons. Weapons instruction starts in the classroom. Trainees learn handgun safety and how officers use a handgun as a "tool" on the job. They handle firearms standing, kneeling, and lying down, and learn to use both their strong and weak hand. Exercises also include firing a gun with obstacles and when lighting conditions are very poor.

Handgun

THINK LIKE A TRAINEE

New recruits seek to impress their teachers and colleagues at police school. Trainees must show they can be both physically and mentally tough, and they can learn a bewildering range of new skills at the same time. Trainees know that if they particularly impress during training, a police department may offer them a job. If they are not offered a job during training, recruits must then look for a job in their local area.

In very competitive situations, it may be a natural response for a person to isolate themselves from their fellow trainees. However, it is important for trainees at the police academy to get to know their classmates. Training schemes reinforce the importance of teamwork because law enforcement is a team-oriented profession.

From the first day of training, cadets will be encouraged to form study groups. Course leaders will also give teams projects and appoint squad leaders, making sure they are rotated so each trainee is given the chance to be squad leader. Police departments achieve better results when officers are able to work well together in teams.

Police academy stresses the importance of gun safety at all times. Guns should be unloaded when not in use; when loaded, the gun should point in a safe direction.

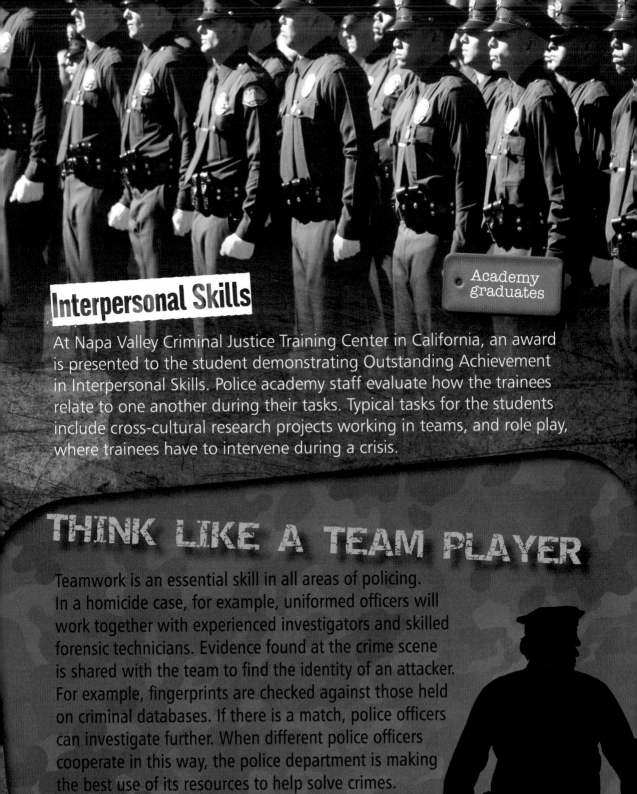

Interpersonal Skills

At Napa Valley Criminal Justice Training Center in California, an award is presented to the student demonstrating Outstanding Achievement in Interpersonal Skills. Police academy staff evaluate how the trainees relate to one another during their tasks. Typical tasks for the students include cross-cultural research projects working in teams, and role play, where trainees have to intervene during a crisis.

Academy graduates

THINK LIKE A TEAM PLAYER

Teamwork is an essential skill in all areas of policing. In a homicide case, for example, uniformed officers will work together with experienced investigators and skilled forensic technicians. Evidence found at the crime scene is shared with the team to find the identity of an attacker. For example, fingerprints are checked against those held on criminal databases. If there is a match, police officers can investigate further. When different police officers cooperate in this way, the police department is making the best use of its resources to help solve crimes.

Could you be a
police trainee?

24

Find out if you have what it takes to join the police force. Use the information you have read so far to answer the following questions:

Q1. Give another name for police school.

Q2. How many weeks does police training usually last?

Q3. Where do recruits spend their time working?

Q4. What is it essential for trainees to be when handling weapons?

Q5. With which hand are recruits trained to fire their guns?

Q6. If trainees particularly impress during training, what might happen?

Q7. Name a type of forensic information found at a crime scene that can be used to find the identity of an attacker.

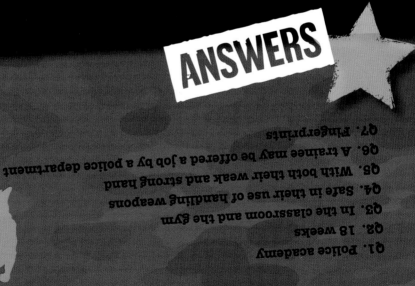

ANSWERS

Q7. Fingerprints
Q6. A trainee may be offered a job by a police department
Q5. With both their weak and strong hand
Q4. Safe in their use of handling weapons
Q3. In the classroom and the gym
Q2. 18 weeks
Q1. Police academy

CHAPTER 4:
Making the Grade

The methods used to hire individuals as police officers vary across the United States. However, all states have similar basic requirements and applicants have to pass a number of tests. The police department will start with a check on the applicant's background to make sure they are suitable to become a police officer. In addition, candidates will have to pass both a physical fitness test and a variety of written, personality, and other psychological tests.

Trainees have to be fit and they must train hard—even in bad weather.

Physical Fitness Test

A medical doctor checks each applicant. Should applicants not have any medical problems, they will then need to complete physical tests. The Physical Qualification Test (PQT) is tough. For the New Jersey State Police (NJSP) PQT, for example, the applicants have to complete the following:

⭐ Running 1.5 miles (2.4 km) in 14 minutes and 26 seconds, or less

⭐ 18 or more push-ups in 2 minutes

⭐ 21 or more sit-ups in 2 minutes

⭐ Completing two trials of the timed 75-yard (69 m) obstacle course

Some PQTs include "the wall" as part of the course. Clearing this 6-foot (1.8 m) barrier at speed is feared by many.

THINK LIKE A NEW RECRUIT

To succeed in their quest to become police officers, young hopefuls will have to demonstrate strength. They will need to show upper-body strength in the demanding physical tests, along with stamina. More than anything, they will need to show perseverance and determination. Police officers must show that they can keep going, even when they are exhausted. This type of attitude can prove that they are mentally strong as well as physically able.

27

Strong Body... Strong Mind

Police force applicants have to pass written examinations that test how well they remember information, as well as their ability to learn and reason. Psychological tests assess the trainees' personality and try to predict whether they have what it takes to be police officers.

Police officers must prove they are mentally strong enough to deal with the pressures of their job, including carrying weapons and entering very dangerous situations.

Strengths and Weaknesses

Police work is tough—and most people will prove not to be at all suited to it. Typical police psychology tests examine a number of key personality features in candidates. Such tests attempt to find out answers to the following questions: How sociable are you? How friendly and kind are you? How organized are you? How calm are you? How creative/curious are you? While there are no right or wrong answers to these questions, certain types of people will be much better suited to police work than others.

Those who show the right personality traits to become police officers also need to be made aware of their strengths and weaknesses. Knowing and understanding these can mean that recruits can focus on their strengths and lessen the impact of their weaknesses in their everyday police work.

THINK LIKE A LAW ENFORCEMENT OFFICER

As part of their psychological testing, candidates are strapped to a polygraph or "lie detector." This machine measures different body functions and reactions, including breathing, blood pressure, and perspiration (sweating). Increases in one or more of these may indicate that a person is lying. The machines are accurate, but not infallible. It is important that candidates give honest answers so that their examiners can build an accurate personality profile. This helps assess if the candidates are truly suitable for a career in police work.

TAKE THE TEST!

Could you make the grade?

Find out if you have the mental strength to be a police officer by recalling the information you have read:

Q1. What does PQT stand for?

Q2. In the NJSP physical qualification test, how far does the applicant have to run in 14 minutes and 26 seconds, or less?

Q3. In the NJSP PQT, how many push-ups does the applicant have to complete in 2 minutes?

Q4. How high is "the wall?"

Q5. What do psychological tests assess?

Q6. What is the polygraph examination commonly known as?

Q7. Name three functions that the polygraph measures.

ANSWERS

Q7. Breathing, blood pressure, and perspiration
Q6. The lie detector test
Q5. A candidate's personality and whether they have what it takes to become a police officer
Q4. 6 feet (1.8 m)
Q3. At least 18 push-ups
Q2. 1.5 miles (2.4 km)
Q1. Physical Qualification Test

CHAPTER 5:
On the Road

When police officers explore a patrol area in their car, they are always on the lookout, either for criminal acts or people who look suspicious. Patrol officers stop cars on the highway for traffic violations, such as a driver running a red light. They may investigate JDLRs, when a situation "just doesn't look right." If police officers investigate a JDLR, they can check out any information provided by the suspect on a criminal database linked to the police car's computer.

A traffic cop carries out a traffic stop, to detain a vehicle in order to check out a possible violation of law.

Crash Scene Incidents

Crash scenes can be particularly difficult to deal with, especially when there are fatalities. Calls to accident scenes require a quick and organized response from police officers. If police officers arrive first at the scene of the crash, officers need to keep calm and work quickly and effectively to make sure that traffic is diverted away from the accident. Often, they will use their own cars as shields to protect the area from other traffic. This will give the patrol officers the chance to check on the injured. Officers need to make quick decisions about injured people and how best to treat them. They may need to give first aid or, if necessary, ask for help from other emergency services, such as emergency medical technicians (EMTs) and firefighters.

Radioing for help

THINK LIKE A TRAFFIC ENFORCEMENT OFFICER

At the scene of a crash, officers seek to find out if one driver has violated the right of way of another, and caused the accident. They also need to establish if the law was broken, for example, had one party been drinking alcohol or using their cell phone while driving? Any witnesses to a car crash need to be interviewed.

Traffic Cops

It is the job of every traffic police officer to make sure that drivers obey traffic laws, such as speed limits. Traffic regulations, enforced by highway patrols, help improve safety on the road. This is not the only job that traffic cops do, however. They have many other duties. Traffic police report damage to the highways, for example, after extreme weather conditions. They also have to deal with serious accidents on the road.

Road Safety

Traffic police need to have a very clear focus at all times. They must carefully monitor what happens on the roads and highways in their region, quickly deal with any issues, and keep people safe. Safety is the number one priority for traffic cops. Both their own safety, and the safety of other road users, always has to be uppermost in their mind.

Traffic cops use sophisticated equipment. They can point a radar gun at a speeding car on a highway to see how fast it is traveling.

In pursuit

Traffic cops need to know how to handle their motorbikes and automobiles at high speeds. They may have to drive fast on the highways to catch law breakers. A high-speed police chase in a movie may seem incredibly exciting, but in reality, police chases involve enormous skill and officers will always be mindful of safe driving and other road users.

THINK LIKE A TRAFFIC COP

Sometimes, traffic police officers go into schools to educate young people about jobs in the police force. They always take care to impress upon students the importance of safe driving as part of their role. When directing traffic—if the lights fail at an intersection, for example—or driving their car in a high-speed chase, police officers must keep themselves safe.

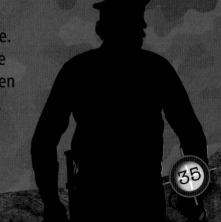

TAKE THE TEST!

Could you be a traffic cop?

Traffic cops need to be observant. Did you pay enough attention to answer these questions correctly?

Q1. What does JDLR stand for?

Q2. What does EMT stand for?

Q3. What should an officer do with police cars at an accident?

Q4. When dealing with injured people, which other emergency services should a police officer work with?

Q5. Of what medical use can a police officer be at an accident?

Q6. What sort of traffic laws must drivers obey?

Q7. If traffic police drive fast, what is the number one priority?

ANSWERS

Q7. Safety

Q6. Speed limits, traffic lights, and not driving under the influence of alcohol or while using a cell phone

Q5. Give first aid if necessary, and if no EMTs are present

Q4. Firefighters and EMTs

Q3. Use them as a shield to protect the crash scene

Q2. Emergency medical technician

Q1. Just doesn't look right

37

CHAPTER 6:
Militarized Police

Tactical teams can be found all over the world in military police forces. Such teams sometimes have to face extreme dangers. They are heavily armed and may protect themselves with shields, as well a armored clothing. Responding to violent situations on the streets or confronting gangs holed up in buildings, military police call-outs can occasionally end in fatal gun-battles. Since 9/11, the threat of terrorism has increased around the world, and the military police need to be able to respond to this.

Thai p
comm

Into Action

Using army-type equipment and uniforms, modern military police officers can look like soldiers. They often wear army-style helmets, fire-retardant balaclavas, and ballistic vests. The weapons they carry include submachine guns, carbines, rifles, and shotguns, including pump-action firearms. Other tactical weapons that they use may include tear gas grenades, which produce a choking smoke that irritates the eyes, and stun grenades, which create a loud noise and blinding light. While good training and equipment is vital, it is most important that military police officers are mentally prepared for action. They will need to be at a heightened state of readiness.

In Mosul, Iraq, a US Army sergeant teaches Iraqi police ways of dealing with riots: always face a hostile crowd.

MP

POLICE

THINK LIKE AN SAS SOLDIER

The Special Air Service (SAS), the United Kingdom's special forces unit, started using stun grenades in the 1970s. Since then, many militarized police forces have continued to use these grenades in raids. The aim of the "flash-bang" technique is to create a blinding light and 160 decibels of noise or more. The unexpected bright light and loud bang will disorientate, or stun, an enemy for a few vital seconds, giving the SAS team an advantage and the ability to disarm the enemy.

Special Weapons and Tactics (SWAT) teams are specialist teams that wear armored clothing and carry a range of firepower. In 1964, the Philadelphia Police Department set up the first SWAT team, boasting a 100-man squad to combat an increase in bank robberies in the city. One of the most famous SWAT teams, the LAPD SWAT team, emerged in 1967 to deal with difficult situations beyond the capabilities of regular police officers.

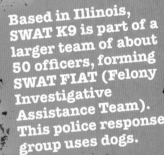

Numbers of heavily armed SWAT teams have soared around the United States over the years. The presence and number of militarized police officers is controversial. Some people are unhappy that officers, dressed and armed like combat troops, act more like soldiers than police officers.

Based in Illinois, SWAT K9 is part of a larger team of about 50 officers, forming SWAT FIAT (Felony Investigative Assistance Team). This police response group uses dogs.

Dealing with Danger

SWAT teams have to face heavy-duty disorders and crime. In many cities, powerful drug lords fight among themselves to protect their territories. Terrorism is also an ever-present danger today. When there is a terrorist attack, the police force must mobilize a large SWAT team with speed and efficiency. Occasionally, they also have to deal with tricky hostage situations. At these times, it is critical that the police make quick and effective decisions.

Military police

THINK LIKE AN LAPD SWAT OFFICER

SWAT call-outs are quite rare. For this reason, SWAT officers carry out regular police duties much of the time. However, they need to be on standby, ready to respond to a SWAT call immediately. On patrol, SWAT members do not wear their armored gear, but they often carry SWAT weapons and equipment secured in their police vehicles, so that they can change quickly into armored clothing and have their weapons to hand if needed.

Militarized Police Around the World

Malaysia's FRU

Around the world, from Italy to India and Malaysia, most countries have their own militarized police forces. One of the most famous of these is Italy's Carabinieri. This militarized police force is older than the country of Italy itself. It was founded more than 200 years ago as the police force of the Kingdom of Sardinia.

The Task Force is the name of Mexico City's elite uniformed police force. This militarized police unit accounts for one-third of the city's 100,000 police officers—making sure the city has one of the lowest crime rates in Mexico.

Rapid Action Force

India's Rapid Action Force (RAF) was formed in 1991, as part of the country's Central Reserve Police Force. Its motto is "Serving Humanity with Sensitive Policing." The RAF deals with riots on the streets, as well as terrorist attacks, such as the November 2008 assaults in Mumbai.

Federal Reserve Unit

Formed almost two years before the country achieved independence in 1957, Malaysia's Federal Reserve Unit (FRU) is a force under the control of the Royal Malaysia Police. The FRU is used chiefly for riot control and other public disorders, but the unit also helps with disaster relief, such as floods.

THINK LIKE A CARABINIERI

The Carabinieri have a dual role in policing Italy—as a police force and as an armed force. Italians are as likely to call the Carabinieri as they are to call the regular state police. Whether they are based in the capital city of Rome or a tiny mountain village, officers in the Carabinieri need to be good with local people. They need to have the ability to operate like a soldier, too.

Carrying riot shields, Carabinieri prepare for the worst when faced with demonstrations.

Have You Got What It Takes?

Do you want to become a police officer?
Following these steps will help you reach your goal.

School

Join teams because teamwork is important to a police officer. Work hard and get good grades so you can go to college.

Keep Fit

Play sports at school. Exercise regularly because police officers have to be fit. Playing team sports also shows that you can work as a member of a team.

Police Academy

Most police officers attend some sort of police academy, where they take physical and written exams to complete their training before they can enter the police force.

College

Completing a degree in criminal justice, law enforcement, or a related subject can help you find work as a police officer. While not required by many police departments, applicants may find a degree helps them find work in the police force.

Behavior

You must have a history of lawful conduct so that you will pass a background check. Your past behavior must show positive features that will support your application to be a police officer.

Work Experience

Work experience prepares you for the long hours and rules that come with being a police officer. You do not have to do a job related to law enforcement, although that may help. Work experience shows that you are responsible and capable of doing a job well.

Volunteer

Volunteering with your local police department is a great place to start. However, volunteering with any community service organization can provide you with some of the skills needed to be a community police officer.

Glossary

ballistic vests body armor that protects the wearer from the impact of bullets

carbines short rifles

combat troops soldiers engaged in fighting

counselors people trained to give help on personal problems

database a set of information, or data, held on a computer

decibels units used to measure the strength of sound

disorientate to confuse

document to record something (in written, photographic, or other form)

domestic relating to or involving someone's home or family

emergency medical technician (EMT) someone trained to do medical work

fatalities deaths

fire-retardant balaclavas headgear made of material that does not easily catch fire

forensics scientific techniques used in crime detection

grenade a small bomb that is designed to be thrown by someone or shot from a rifle

homicide murder

hostage a person captured and held by another

infallible incapable of being wrong

intelligence knowledge about a criminal's methods and motives

lethal force deadly force, or force used that may result in the death of another person

mobilize to prepare troops for service

polygraph a lie detector test

recruit a person beginning their training

tactical showing careful planning toward a specific military end

terrorism the use of violence to pursue certain political aims

violated broken the rules

For More Information

Books

Bowman, Chris. *Police Officer* (Dangerous Jobs). Minneapolis, MN: Bellwether Media, 2014.

Herweck, Diana. *All in a Day's Work: Police Officer* (Time for Kids Nonfiction Readers). Huntington Beach, CA: Teacher Created Materials, 2013.

Laughlin, Kara L. *Police Dogs* (Service Dogs). North Mankato, MN: Child's World, 2014.

Spilsbury, Louise. *Police Officer* (Careers That Count). New York, NY: PowerKids Press, 2015.

Websites

For much more information about the LAPD, log on at:
www.lapdonline.org

The Napa Valley Criminal Justice Training Center in California has information about training to be a police officer at:
www.nvccjtc.com

This website from Toronto Police Service is packed with helpful information and includes a user-friendly section called Kids' Safety Zone at:
www.torontopolice.on.ca/safetyzone

Index